CONTENTS

INTRODUCTION

Entrepreneurship is a journey; it takes hard work and a lot of risk-taking. It is a process that precludes instant gratification. For any course of action, there are undergirds that make things work. They are the tools, resources, or foundation indispensable to the entirety of a process. Habits, which are repetitive behaviors or actions, have a bearing on whatever we do. They are often described as having the power to "make or break us."

Peculiar ways of feeling, thinking, or willing can be instrumental in running an enterprise or startups. Usually, previous mental experiences have to be repeated to acquire these thought processes and actions.

This book is a guide on the ten habits for highly effective entrepreneurs.

CHAPTER 1

RISE EARLY

My ears get the proverbial perk up when I'm privy to seeing or hearing information centered on helping me get the best out of my sleep or nap time. Usually, I don't mind if it involves restructuring my schedule and probably sleeping early. This is precisely why I was open-minded about the idea of having to rise early the first time I heard about it. When talks of sleep sessions, wake time, and afternoon naps come up, its most often posed a peculiar way. Usually, it's the early birds/larks placed side by side the night owls for comparison. Then, individuals randomly state how well their regular or irregular sleeping patterns work for them.

Sleeping is a natural and biological activity that humans, as well as animals, participate in. This natural way in which the human body repairs itself may seem ordinary to us, so much so that its importance is dismissed. Timeliness, too, is often overlooked, and a lot of persons do not know that it is best to have a fixed pattern of sleep with an average of 8 hours during the night for adults.

I would consider myself an avid hard worker. I was the type to get carried away with the day's job so much that it would spill over into nighttime. Other times, it didn't have to be work, but it still kept me up late. It was much like a negative feedback loop, centered on keeping me unproductive while still preventing me from enjoying my sleep.

So, what is the "Rise Early," mantra, or principle all about? The Rise Early principle gets to you to make the most out of your day by making certain adjustments. Just as it appears, it involves rising early. Research has shown that humans make more accurate decisions during the early hours of the day. From 8 am to 1 pm, we are better able to maximize our decision-making ability, although we tend to take more time to make these decisions.

Asides better decision-making abilities, being an early riser has multifarious rewards. A study published in 2019 by Nature Communications, indicates that those who wake up early due to the nature of their genes are less at risk of being schizophrenic or depressed. Not everyone identifies as an early riser. However, there are quite a lot of early bird benefits to be harnessed.

Why should you rise early?

Keep the aforementioned biological benefits of being an early bird in mind. Now, imagine that you get to be deliberate about when you sleep and your ability to rise early, so much so that it becomes a habit. First, you likely get more time to prepare yourself for the next day's work. Deciding to settle in early puts you in a position to make sure that you get everything all set for the next day, most times with a clear blueprint in mind. It becomes a slow and deliberate process.

You are also more likely to want to enjoy the average recommended hours of sleep through the night if you decide to rise early. As individuals, we can probably relate to the crankiness that comes along with having an inadequate sleep or being disturbed while trying to get some sleep. Lack of sleep or sleep deprivation has various debilitating effects, and the sleep foundation recommends seven to nine hours of night sleep for adults, although individual needs may vary.

Over the last decade, scientific research has indicated strong links between poor sleep and higher body weight in humans, depression, higher calorie intake, increased inflammation, and a higher risk for stroke and heart diseases.

The circadian rhythm is a 24-hour cycle that is a part of the body's internal clock. Its roles as related to sleep are vital, and a well-known circadian rhythm is the sleep-wake cycle. As humans, our bodies' systems usually depend on circadian rhythms coordinated by what is referred to as the "master clock" present in our brains. Environmental signals, particularly light, have a significant level of direct influence on the master clock. This is why the circadian rhythm remains tied to the cycle of day and night.

It is usually much harder for most individuals to get daytime worth of sleep for the recommended hours. This may occur due to natural interference from the circadian system or jarring and unpredictable environmental disturbance.

Tips on how to rise early.

To get your body prepared for the task ahead, your mind must be at the ideal place. Here are a few tips on rising early.

Scheduling

Scheduling involves preparing a pre-bedtime and morning routine. Early risers are known for getting the work done and are less likely to procrastinate compared to night owls. First, you have to decide when to sleep and form a routine around it. Then, set an ideal wake time. To optimize the early rise process, line up activities for that period as it helps to prevent any form of lag.

This tip is essential to rising early because it is a deliberate effort targeted at modifying the sleep-wake cycle.

- **Do it gradually**

Being able to sleep and wake at a designated time does not just happen out of the blue. It is a gradual process that the body is eased into. Newbie early risers often make the mistake of setting the precise time they have chosen to wake at first. Think about how jarring it will be for a body that is yet to adapt to this modified cycle?

For a more effective experience, be gradual about it. At first, do not set your newly preferred wake up time. Instead, dial your current wake up time by 30 minutes at most, and then move down gradually from there. Naturally, if you are religious about it, your body's very likely to pick up on these cues and go along with it.

- **Optimize your experience with technology.**

Asides drawing the curtains and shutting off all forms of light before sleep, light, and smart alarms are innovative devices that work by capitalizing on science and technology. Remember the brain's master clock, and how light has a significant level of direct influence on it? This fact can be harnessed for a better experience.

Light alarms work by simulating the natural sunrise. On the other hand, smart alarms track your sleeping cycle and utilize this information to wake you when you are in light sleep. This way, you get the optimal amount of sleep, and you are less likely to want to jump back to bed as soon as you wake.

- **Accountability factor.**

You do not want to be fueled by willpower alone. Sometimes, willpower fails. So, you need all the support you can get from your partner, friends, and family. Support in this sense involves being held accountable by the standards, and schedules set. Having someone, you would not want to disappoint, confirm that you are true to your routine, and the activities in your plans provide many benefits. You are more likely to go through with it, with or without innate willpower being present.

What to do when you rise early.

1. **Exercise**

Think about it. You probably only get to hit the gym on your free day or weekends. If you are not a remote worker, it is very likely that you get too tired to do a bit of exercise after work. Fixing in exercise into regular morning routine has very many advantages. Exercise is known to increase alertness, improve focus, and mood.

A study published in 2019 by the British Journal of Sports Medicine indicates that morning exercise improves visual attention, visual learning, and decision-making. Set up your routine around the four primary types of exercise; endurance exercises, strength, balance, and flexibility focused exercise. It is absolutely essential that you get the different benefits peculiar to each kind, and not be biased to one.

Endurance or aerobic exercises involve the full use of oxygen. These tend to increase breathing rates as well as heart rates. The benefits of this type of training include improved fitness and heart health. Aerobic exercises include activities as simple as brisk walking or jogging. Swimming is also a type of aerobic exercise.

Strength focused exercise aims to build muscular strength. Strong muscles play a part in keeping the human body balanced and averting injuries that deal with imbalance, such as falling. Strength focused exercise includes activities like lifting weights or making use of resistance bands.

Balanced focused exercise also aims to prevent balance-related problems such as falling. While this is more common amongst older people, it should not be excluded from your routine. Balance centered exercise includes activities such as; The heel to toe walk or switching between balancing on one foot or the other.

Flexibility centered exercises focus on building up body flexibility. This is done mainly by stretching, and examples of these forms of practice include the ankle stretch exercise or calf stretch exercise.

The importance of exercise cannot be overemphasized. This is why I advise that you create a routine around these basic types of work out. It is recommended that you seek advice from an expert before going all out. With the help of an expert, you are more likely to get a well-structured routine, and the best out of your morning exercise.

2. SELF-CARE

Self-care is indispensable and should go on whether or not you identify as an early riser. It involves activities like grooming, meditation, and even overlooked aspects like not skipping breakfast. Self-care is simply caring for one's self. It is multifaceted as it involves balancing and optimizing both personal as well as professional commitments. So, it concerns the physical, mental, emotional, and spiritual.

Clearly, self-care goes past the materialistic and consumer-centric agenda pushed by a lot of brands out there. It does not mean grooming should be dismissed, only that other aspects of self-care should not be less focused on, or considered relatively unimportant. To get on the right track, it is essential that you create a self-care plan.

The Self-care plan

Self-care can be described as any deliberate act aimed at improving physical, mental and emotional health. It puts "self" into focus, aids stress management and helps improve general well-being. With a self-care plan, it is much easier to understand the concept of self-care. It catalyzes the process of developing and setting ideas related to self-care in motion. To make this work, you must choose the essential aspects of your life and apply effective strategies. Below are some tips and effective strategies.

- **Physical self-care plan.**

Physical self-care is focused on the physical and how actions done physically can improve general well-being. This self-care plan is focused on the human body. There is a strong connection between the body and the mind. Certain activities involving the body have also been discovered to improve overall health while keeping people in the right mind state.

Create a plan for these activities. These include exercising, grooming, maintaining a regular sleep routine, eating a healthy diet, and breakfast. Breakfast is regarded as an essential meal of the day. Most people do not naturally identify as the breakfast type, although there are lots of rewards attached to starting the day off with a healthy breakfast.

Over the years, research has shown a connection between eating breakfast and improved memory as well as concentration. It is also linked to good health. It is somewhat easy to get cranky without breakfast. Just as it sounds, breakfast breaks a night long fast and serves to replenish dwindling energy. It is the best type of head start.

- **Mental self-care plan**

As humans, our mentality, the way we think and things we occupy our minds with, can greatly influence our psychological wellbeing. An ideal mental self-care plan should consist of mentally stimulating activities which are critical to staying mentally healthy. Examples of these types of activities include studying, exploring curious topics, watching movies or playing intelligent games such as puzzles.

Other useful practices that can help tune out the inner critic and foster healthy internal dialogue are self-compassion and self-acceptance.

- **Emotional self-care plan.**

Emotions are vital and should be acknowledged. As humans, when we consciously or subconsciously choose not to address any of the emotions we feel, or bottle up our feelings, we become more prone to stress and anxiety. These two are known, productivity killers. This is why it is important to explore all kinds of emotions safely, regardless of how tumultuous they are. Here are some tips on building an ideal emotional self-care plan.

Develop great relationships.

Socialization is vital to self-care. Be deliberate about developing great friendships; keep your family and friends close. Ensure that you have a working support system and play a supportive role in these relationships.

Keep a journal.

Journals are useful for reflective purposes. At the end of each day, you can write gratitude or happy lists in your journal. As humans, we are often too occupied by the numerous negative thoughts swirling around our heads. Negative emotions usually have a way of making small feats achieved for the day. Sometimes, a little reminder of positive highlights can be all that's needed to make you feel better.

Do things that make you happy.

Happiness is stress relieving and involves the release of dopamine as well as other vital hormones. Aside from being able to combat stress, doing things that make you happy can be critical in diminishing the rote effect. Rote diminishing activities include participating in sports, games, and hobbies. It could also involve doing things as simple as seeing a movie.

Spiritual self-care plan.

Spiritual self-care is purpose centric, meaningful, and imbued in the sense of sacredness. It aims to achieve clarity and as well as a feeling of oneness with the universe. The concept of what is considered spiritual and profound greatly differs across individuals. Spirituality can be associated with the esoteric, age-old traditions, nature, or religion. For some, spirituality can be found in vehicles of expression such as music, dance, and art. Here are some tips on making the best out of a spiritual self-care plan.

Practice meditation.

Meditation can be broken down into different forms depending on its purpose. Common types of mediation include mantra, mindfulness, spiritual, focused, transcendental, and movement meditation. This wellness practice involving both the body and mind has both physical and mental benefits.

Meditation is known to reduce stress, improve focus, as well as concentration. To practice mediation, seek a mediation expert or try out a well-reviewed mediation app. There are also several meditations centered resources online that would be quite useful.

Be mindful.

Mindfulness is often mentioned in stoic themed philosophies. To put it simply, it involves genuinely living in the present moment and being aware. It is the opposite of being far away from ourselves and living in autopilot mode. Mindfulness has been reported to reduce stress and anxiety and is also cited as necessary for happiness. To practice mindfulness, engage in mindfulness meditation, or take a mindful walk. The purpose here is to bring to focus the present and live in the current moment.

Free your mind, enjoy the fresh air out, soak yourself in the great ambiance of a decluttered space, observe your surroundings, and nourish your senses.

Journaling.

Journaling is a reflective and intentional activity that makes individuals more mindful of their routine. Writing is regarded as a means of expression which sifts through and addresses specific thoughts or emotions. Keeping a journal can be cathartic, and would make a great addition to a spiritual self-care plan.

Making the best out of your day.

I find rising early wholly in sync with utmost preparedness for the day, especially when effective routines back it up. To make the best out of your day, preparation cannot be dismissed. This involves creating a habit of useful morning and evening routines, as well as meeting daily goals. In the next chapter, we take a look at another productive habit; goal setting.

CHAPTER 2

SET GOALS

Entrepreneurs, business owners, and companies generally work with targets or clear indicators that usually signal profit or loss. These are typically defined by percentages, profit margins, market shares, or revenue generated. Goal setting involves committing oneself to achieve short or long-term objectives, often by utilizing deadlines and clear, quantifiable measures. Primarily, business and personal goals should be set. These goals usually go hand in hand and contribute to overall growth.

Goals are envisioned ideas for the future or specific desired results that individuals commit to achieving typically within a clearly stated, finite period. Usually, particular characteristics of a goal help in defining it; these characteristics, to an extent, also indicate the level of motivation an individual possesses to accomplish these goals. For example, the importance of a goal can be rated either low or high. On the other hand, the difficulty level of a goal is a characteristic that can be gauged by estimating the likelihood of accomplishing that goal.

Specificity, temporal range, level of consciousness, and complexity are other distinct features of goals. Specificity relates to whether a target is well defined; a goal is either vague or precisely defined. The temporal range describes both the finite period set for a purpose, as well as how soon it can be accomplished. Level of consciousness relates to the extent of awareness possessed by an individual on goals set. Naturally, we are more likely to be cognitively aware of goals that are proximally more achievable compared to farther ones.

Complexity describes connectivity between goals and is determined by the number of mini-goals required to achieve a single primary goal.

Why should you have or set goals?

- **Excellent source of motivation.**

A clearly defined goal is an excellent source of motivation. Having a critical objective next in line to be accomplished is a great way to keep you geared up. This usually works because goal setting keeps an envisioned idea or desired result in focus.

- **It allows for thoughtful introspection on what is truly important.**

The process of goal setting involves deep thinking about what is regarded as important in personal life or business. It also includes having to come to terms with the answers to the big questions associated with several aspects of life. When the deep thinking is done, what remains are end desires that have to be accomplished. These are then broken down into attainable and measurable goals.

- **Focus**

Think about how chaotic our lives would be as humans if we lacked clearly defined goals? Goals are purposeful and can give direction while allowing tasks to be efficiently performed. With clearly defined goals set, it is also less probable that time and effort will be wasted.

What are short term goals?

These goals have short timespans and are relatively closer to the future than other types of goals. They are connected to and link up much bigger objectives. Short term goals give regular and continuous bursts of motivation because of their relatively short duration. Usually, I find that it is more efficient to break a long-term goal into smaller objectives. Short term goals or STG's are often achievable within twelve months or less.

STG's can be focused on career, personal life, health, finance, or academics.

What are long term goals?

Long term goals are farther into the future and more long-term compared to short term goals. They are accomplished over time, usually with the aid of short-term goals. These goals require strategic planning and focus because they tend to happen later in life. A long-term goal can be divided into lifetime and capstone goals. "Lifetime" indicates that long-term goal tends to span across an individual's life, typically coming to completion in later years.

These goals cut across different areas of life and are not restricted to finances, career, education, or family. Lifetime goals often start out as general but become more directional and specific as time goes by. Capstone goals, on the other hand, are those goals that have to be accomplished first before lifetime goals. Think of them as milestones on a road map or checkpoints on roads that simply indicate arrival at a designated point.

The ability to be intentional is critical in the quest to achieving long term goals. I make this work by working backward to achieve my goals. It has worked quite well for me so far.

backward to me involves a visceral mental
and thought process. It works because it places
in the exact mind or mental state, they would
possess to accomplish their goals, although this
briefly. It is also effective because it focuses on
truly essential to make a goal or vision work.

a lot to be said about writing things down. Writing
visions or goals allows for reflection and sharper
g. Most often, I find that I am able to express my
ts and verbalize my intentions better. When a goal
on is written down first, it becomes much easier to
backward. The process becomes seamless and more
tive.

y individuals don't get farther than intending to
eve mind-based resolutions. However, being deliberate
writing things can provide the needed much clarity and
rease the likelihood of goals being achieved. A lot of
idence continues to point out the various benefits of
ngaging in this activity. Research published by

How to be intentional; working backward to reach set goals.

Being intentional involves living life by design and not by default. Choosing to live intentionally precludes operating on autopilot. Instead, it involves making decisions and being deliberate about what goes on in your life. We are not in control of the variables that the universe subsists on. It's quite impossible to be that powerful, as this would involve being in control of everyone around us and nature, both of which are inherently unpredictable.

This is why I subscribe to the stoic philosophy as the perfect guide for making life work amongst the uncertainty. It is intentional and involves navigating the universe with vital qualities such as reason, mindfulness, practical wisdom, and self-control. Here are some tips on being intentional.

- **Write your Vision.**

When I write, I tend to create a blueprint out of it. For me, it goes further than merely iterating my goals or vision. I usually take it a step further by doing what I refer to as

"Working backward". N

down a long-term goal. A

deciding to live healthy af

financial goal, on the othe

business.

To apply the principle of

previous objective, I would de

do scientists consider to be he

cutting down calories, ditching

vegetables into my diet, or exerci

penned down after deep thinkin

thing to do is address, "losing 25 po

To do this, I would picture my he

pounds' loss body. How do I look, ar

me to get there? Are there habits I cur

would undermine the progress made

weight loss body? That's the best pl

There's always a target, the desired re

perfect picture in mind first, when workin

Working

experienc

individual

need to

happens

what is

There's

down

thinkin

thoug

or vis

work

effec

Mar

ach

and

inc

ev

e

psychological science has shown that writing by hand helps to process information better. It also has strong connections to improved focus and better memory.

In terms of goal setting, writing things down has also been discovered to increase productivity. This works because this activity puts you in the mind space to focus on what's really important. People who write down their goals or visons have been reported to be 1.2 to 1.4 times more likely to accomplish them compared to those who do not write it.

- **Be Proactive**

Proactivity is synonymous with being forward-looking. It involves acting in advance and being deliberate about dealing with unforeseen changes or difficulties. It is often juxtaposed with being "reactive," and the word reactive usually precludes premeditation. There are tell-tale signs of being the reactive type; people who are reactive are not likely to make decisions based on their values, principles, or deep thinking. These individuals are more likely to be caught off guard, are often acted upon, and do not possess the mental agency to extricate stimulus from response.

On the other hand, proactive people prepare and make plans, ceteris paribus. However, these individuals also have other back up strategies just in case things do not happen to fall in place, or work as planned. This simply means that proactive people tend to respond better to situations as they are not likely to be caught off guard.

Proactivity has several rewards; this take-charge attitude and mentality is very anti-stress and rightly so. Think about it, things are certainly less stressful without procrastination, and a proactive person is not likely to procrastinate.

Procrastination has been described as a self-regulated type of failure involving the unnecessary delay of activities regardless of the subsequent adverse effects that may come along with it. It is linked to lower self-esteem, lower levels of self-compassion, and higher levels of neuroticism. Individuals who anticipate problems, and continuously seek a bull by the horn approach to situations, get the job done.

They are also less likely to be plagued by anxiety. Here are some tips on being proactive: -

Work with daily tasks and to-do lists.

These are essential because they narrow the scope of what is necessary for the day. Daily goals should be defined first at the start of the day. These goals should then be broken down into smaller tasks with the aid of a "to-do list." Items iterated in a to-do list should be prioritized, with more essential activities ranked above less important ones. These activities can be divided into morning, afternoon, and evening objectives.

To make this process more effective, employ the use of scheduling. Scheduling should not have to translate to inflexibility in daily activities. The use of a schedule should simply serve to emphasize the fact that timing is crucial when planning daily tasks. When events are prioritized and timed, there is a more definite sense of direction.

Be prepared.

For efforts to be effective and a hundred percent, preparedness is essential. Preparation involves being geared up to face whatever's coming. Doing this requires taking cognizance of the current situation and being able to predict what might happen next.

Taking on challenges and efficiently addressing them requires a level of mental and sometimes emotional preparedness. In the next chapter, we discuss building these two.

CHAPTER 3

STUDY

Acquiring knowledge about a subject matter or topic typically involves studying or listening. Academics popularly use the word study in combination with words like "for," which indicates that people study for a particular reason. Why do student's study? Students primarily study to ace tests or exams. Also, higher-paying jobs usually require a higher level of dedication to studying in order to gain the necessary expertise. However, studying isn't only for people who are involved in academics.

As a non-academic, are there also benefits to studying?

When we study, we increase our current level of understanding, the knowledge we possess, and our access to opportunities. Those who do not study might be curious but simply do nothing about exploring their curiosities. In the ever-dynamic and increasingly progressive world that we live in today, such inactions seem tantamount to regression as it cuts off the innate human ability to develop and evolve. Most often, when most people hear the word studying, they picture libraries inundated with books and lamps by the bedside reading table.

However, since studying involves acquiring knowledge on a subject to apply it in practice, it is not restricted to traditional definitions of learning. While we can study by experimental research, we acquire knowledge by learning from previous experiences too. People who study habitually gain lifelong rewards that include expanded awareness and a greater understanding of themselves.

Asides from these, people who study also have a lot to talk about as they are often well informed. Studying is also linked to increased confidence in one's abilities.

When I'm not reading academic books, I'm biased to history and biographies because I learn more from them than other genres or sub-genres. What I do is script out my study targets and have them clearly defined before the beginning of a month. So, before the start of a month, I select a theme and pick books that align with them. Then, I create a schedule littered with incentives, bolstered with a clear deadline.

Usually, I'm too busy enjoying the book selected and acquiring new information to remember these incentives. It does not do a lot of good to stick to the myth that studying only benefits academics or people who need to pass or ace tests.

Reading and Listening.

Reading is a mentally stimulating process involving the interpretation of written language. This cognitive process involves decoding to get meaning from text. It is a form of communication that is used to share information and ideas. It has been reported to increase knowledge, improve memory, focus as well as concentration. Technology has made things much more accessible; nowadays, people read online and digitally via eBooks.

Listening, on the other hand, involves paying attention to a sound or speech. The main difference between hearing and listening is the attention factor. For communication to be effective, appropriate language has to be used; ideas also have to be clear, informal, and consistent.

However, how effective are all of those if the receiver fails to listen?

My favorite quote on listening is by Stephen covey, "Most people do not listen with the intent to understand; they listen with the intent to reply." There are many benefits of effective or active listening. It is indispensable to leadership; when we listen to understand, we can change our perspective about things and challenge previous assumptions. Active listening also helps to resolve conflicts, build and strengthen teamwork as well as inspire people.

What other perks are associated with active listening? Employers are better able to make critical decisions when they get all the necessary facts first. Consider how ineffective it is to simply jump to conclusions or make grand business decisions based on mere assumptions. People have a better shot at making well-informed decisions when they listen.

Consider why active listening would be vital to building teamwork? When team players feel like their contributions are appreciated and noted, it tends to produce a ripple effect. Clearly, it's almost impossible to recognize the ideas, actions, and contributions of others without listening.

To listen better, be deliberate about it. Pay attention and don't zone out or busy yourself thinking about probable counter-arguments. Be present, receptive, and open to the message that's been communicated. Show that you are listening by way of body language and feedback. Avoid assumptions or judgments, and then respond appropriately.

Why should you invest in yourself?

Investing in oneself simply translates to putting the required work in, for improvement and growth to happen.

Investing involves spending time, money, energy, or other resources on something, usually for some benefit or purpose. In the dynamic and ever-changing world that is the twenty-first century, the need for constant introspection and self-development should not be debated. Skills and expertise usually need to be upgraded because previously regarded solutions become outdated as time goes by.

It is not said often, but investing in oneself shouldn't be regarded only as an avenue to move along with the zeitgeist. It goes farther than that. The word "invest" has a ripple effect, which eventually tells on people around us. Leaders, business owners, employers, and CEOs can capitalize on that because it is quite difficult to give what you do not have.

There are some preconceptions about choosing to invest in oneself. It is far from being selfish. As independent beings, we usually have to make the tough decisions ourselves. Typically, the after-effects of the decisions or their consequences are left for us to deal with.

Our choices affect others, too, be it at the workplace or in our personal relationships. As individuals, we spend more time facing the consequences of our decisions alone than facing it with other people. So, it becomes our responsibility to make sure things work.

The word invest isn't restricted to finances, and my go-to advice with matters related to investing mainly focuses on outputs such as; well-being, productivity, and revenue. To me, this multifaceted approach breaks things down and isn't biased to an area of life. Investing would not be as efficient as it should be if it is not all-round. Take, for example, focusing on upgrading previously learned skills and improving prospects of increasing finances while neglecting health and well-being. The probable results? Poor health or burnout.

In this chapter, we take a look at how to invest using the multifaceted approach.

1. **Productivity & revenue.**

The productivity and revenue aspect of this approach is centered on investing in oneself in order to get the best out of business or the workplace. Here are some tips on making it work.

Learn your craft.

Learn your craft, acquire the much-needed skills, get new certifications, and further your degree. I mentioned earlier that the world is dynamic. Most of what we do in the world now is optimized by constantly upgraded technology. It's only natural to want to be progressive and move along with the flow. One good way to make this process more efficient is via mentorship. With a mentor, there's a clearer path in front to follow. There are also lesser chances of making common mistakes.

A lot more benefits come along with standing on the shoulders of giants, as Isaac Newton puts it. The process involved in learning and mastering a craft includes committing to goals, leveraging support systems, and constant practice. To gain expertise, the ten thousand hours rules hold. It simply shows that a lot of time has to be devoted to progressing, adapting to the zeitgeist, and gaining more information or knowledge.

Teaching is another great avenue to learn. It reinforces prior knowledge and then provides the opportunity for previously unknown ideas to be considered.

By teaching, experts in a particular field are also able to impart what they know. Community-based programs are an excellent place to start.

Get coaching.

Coaching is the act by which an individual is coached. When an individual is coached, he or she is trained or instructed on a subject matter. Coaching works because it changes an individual's internal thought process. It focuses on improving the capabilities of high potential performers. From professional athletes to employees or graduates, anybody can get coached. Asides from professional coaches, there are leadership coaches, health, and wellness as well as personal growth coaches, to mention a few. It is not restricted to the workplace.

Where can coaching take place? Before the coaching industry began to unravel, most of this activity took place in what I would refer to as "traditional settings." These include private and individual sessions as well as workshops, which serve as an avenue for a group focused coaching to take place. Now, technology has made things much more accessible, and there are almost no barriers. Coaching can take place on the phone as well as in virtual, visual online sessions.

According to reports from the International Coach Federation, ICF, eighty percent of coached individuals had increased self-confidence. Seventy percent also reported paybacks, such as improved relationships, better work performance, and practical communication skills.

Well-being.

- **Invest in your health.**

The body is much like a vehicle that drives individuals to their different destinations. Would it be an efficient option to drive an unfueled or unpowered car? It wouldn't, and that's precisely why health is a critical topic that has to be paid a lot of attention. Great health plays an indispensable role in our day to day activities. It is almost impossible to go wrong with deliberate and effective health investments.

Nowadays, asides from being bombarded by "living fit and healthy" ads and mantras, the weightiness of medical expenses reminds us of the consequences of certain lifestyle choices. Individuals who have poor health are more likely to spend on healthcare costs. Poor health is also linked to lower life expectancy. Terrible lifestyle choices may lead to savings being wiped out, and hospital bills are accrued or incurred daily. It is sad a road to financial devastation.

On the other hand, individuals who invest in their health have more time to spend with their loved ones and are less at risk of developing diseases associated with unhealthy lifestyle choices. For me, investing in my health would involve making decisions such as having an active lifestyle, getting vital sleep time, ditching unhealthy habits, exercising, and eating the right food types. It could also include getting a health coach.

Health coaches are able to make things work by focusing on the health and wellness of clients via a holistic approach. A health coach is much like a health mentor. With this kind of arrangement, individuals have the freedom to express thoughts and fears about their health. Health coaches understand that people generally have different emotional, lifestyle, and physical needs.

So, they are careful enough to avoid peddling a single cure to various peculiar problems. Instead, they work with their clients by helping them discover the healthiest and most improved version of themselves. Nowadays, health and wellness coaches bridge the gap between patients and doctors.

- **Invest in personal relationships.**

The importance of family and other personal relationships cannot be overlooked. A lot of people get caught up while trying to advance their career or profession. These individuals often end up drifting farther away from their support systems. It takes a lot to manage both career and family. To make it work, be intentional about things.

Proper time management is vital. It's hard to create time for other people when you find it challenging to take some time out yourself. Make plans, and don't be afraid of having to say no to work if you need to.

CHAPTER 4

MEDITATE

Meditation is a practice where people use specific techniques, thoughts, or activities to train attention or awareness. These techniques (such as mindfulness or intense focus on an object) or tools are used to achieve a mentally clear, emotionally calm, and stable state. Meditation can be religious or spiritual, and there are two primary forms; the focused(concentrative) and the open monitoring(mindfulness).

Meditation has many benefits; stress reduction is an advantage of constant meditation that has been proven by science. This practice has been discovered to reduce the symptoms in people who experience medical conditions triggered by stress. Reports from a study that spanned eight weeks indicate that open-monitoring meditation can reduce the inflammation response caused by stress. Reduced stress usually correlates with reduced anxiety.

Mindfulness meditation has also been reported to decrease depression.

Other benefits of this practice include improved sleep, decreased blood pressure, improved emotional health, increased well-being, peace, and perception, to mention a few.

Meditation Tips

Seek guidance

For most, meditation is an unexplored terrain and having a guiding hand would be beneficial. In whatever practice, it is essential to get the basics and foundation correct. This is why having a meditation coach, or a qualified instructor would be apt.

There are also workshops, classes or meditation retreats that will provide the basic information on getting started.

Create the atmosphere

The first tip I got was centered on structuring an ideal daily meditation routine, with five to ten minutes dedicated to this practice. This was after I had decided the right type of meditation for me. The next thing I did was figure out the perfect spot. During meditation, ambiance matters a lot, and the immediate surroundings will have a bearing on your ability to focus. Startlingly bright light, clutter and other distractions can dampen meditation experience. Think of how difficult it would be to begin practicing focused meditation in a noisy location? Exactly.

People who have their meditation space situated around or in their homes find it more comfortable in the long run. It is this way because, forming a habit out of it becomes seamless, along with regular home-related routines. In terms of the right choice of setting, gardens, holy places, and locations that are close to mother nature (fountains, rivers, and streams) are ideal for meditation.

To make for an everyday experience, it is advisable that you select a room within your home. If it was previously occupied, declutter it. While decluttering is often associated with the minimalist movement, it is essential to meditation. During the process of decluttering, remove all kinds of invasive items. Digital devices often fall into this category, especially phones. Primarily, invasive things are those that are not needed, which usually take up unnecessary space.

Invasiveness is not limited to objects within that location. Humans can be invasive too. Roommates, children and family members can be guilty. This is why, I make sure that my family is aware of my meditation schedule. While I cannot control all the variables, for example, noise from neighbors or passing cars, I do my best to make sure I have control of what occurs in my internal world.

This designated location should not be shielded from sunlight, too; it should have a natural feel to it. If the space does not open out to the field, open-air, or green grass, plants or flowers will make a great addition.

Mindset matters

Mindset matters; many people choose not to meditate because they feel that "it's too hard," and it "only starts to pay off after several years." It's pretty common to hear excuses like "meditation is boring" or "I don't have time to meditate." This way of thinking, attitude, or opinion, especially when it has become ingrained and habitual, affects our ability to commit to this practice. Usually, it is because the process becomes riddled with doubts and skepticism.

I find it amazing that people are also quick to disregard the science-backed fact that meditation can change the ingrained mindset and nurture the brain. Change your mindset, and be more open-minded. Approach meditation with an open mind, and get physical, mental, and emotional benefits.

Get centered

To get centered, I go to my designated meditation spot. However, I'm usually premeditative before starting my meditation routine. If there are things that have to be handled before I begin to meditate, I get them done. This way, I am less likely to be distracted during the process. To get in position, I sit upright. The go-to feeling that should accompany that is being comfortable and relaxed, and not being overtly tensed up.

Alignment and extreme focus.

Alignment refers to the proper structuring of the body during mediation. For the best experience, the body and mind have to be aligned. Most often, the basic elements of top meditations postures tend to get tweaked to suit individual taste. However, here are some vital alignment tips for you before you begin to meditate.

- Sit

- Elongate your spine

- Place your hands in a resting position.

- Keep your shoulders relaxed

- Tuck in your chin

- Relax your jaw

- Finally, rest your gaze.

In concentrative meditation, focusing is vital. It's just as it sounds, although your mind might wander and thoughts might ultimately distract you, extreme focus will bring your attention back to your object of focus. There are two primary ways to make this work.

i)   Focus on each inhale or exhale

ii)   Practice extreme focus with a body scan.

When I practice extreme focus with a body scan, I focus intensely on individual parts of my body. First, I begin from my toes, pause, and then feel every sensation. Then, I move up my body from there. Concentrative meditation techniques such as the body scan and the "inhale, exhale routine" have a way of connecting the body and the mind.

Affirmations

Repeat positive statements or phrases during meditation. These are usually referred to as affirmations. They do a lot of good by dispelling reoccurring negative thoughts. When I practice affirmation, I make sure to set the ambiance by playing some meditation music first. As soon as it begins, I meditate while visualizing the statements and phrases I plan to reinforce. I do this for an average of twenty minutes per session. Practice positive affirmations with meditation and feel the positivity soak into your subconscious.

Seek clarity

Guided meditation is my go-to source for clarity. With it, I experience a sense of calm, comfort, and confidence. I find that I am better able to solve complex issues without feeling any of the typical mental drain. This type of meditation is mindfulness focused, intending to keep you in the present moment, and in a calm and relaxed state. It is precisely what you'd need to be able to make effective decisions amidst the chaos of the urban world.

CHAPTER 5

TIMELINESS

This is a habit that everyone should learn. Timeliness should not be regarded as exclusive to some specific kinds of people, say, employees, or students who have to meet up with class. At some point or the other, we would all have to show up or make sure that some work is done well, regardless of our status.

Timeliness refers to the state of being timely. It involves promptness and includes things being done at the proper time. It is characterized by effective time management, readiness, preparedness, as well as confidence. It can be juxtaposed with being poorly timed or ill-timed, root causes of which include lack of regard for people, procrastination, and poor time management.

Tips on timeliness

Figure out why.

The first step to take should be sorting out the "why" question. This aims to address the possible root causes of lateness and doing this helps with providing likely solutions to the problem. There are various reasons why people become perennially late. Some people are absent minded and quick to forget important things; these kinds of people must enlist the use of reminders and notifications when brainstorming possible solutions.

Some get swamped up with unrelated tasks and get easily distracted, while for others, bad habits are culpable. In all, figuring out the why serves to point you in the right direction as to providing likely solutions to the lateness problem.

Break bad habits

In my opinion, people casually disregard time and the importance of timing, and this is a bad habit. Bad habits are debilitating. One psychological phenomenon that proves this casual and almost natural disregard for time is the "planning fallacy". The planning fallacy indicates that people tend to underestimate the extent of time needed for a particular task or activity to be accomplished. According to research, individuals who fall prey of this fallacy, form their opinions based on a skewed and optimistic view of the past.

You do not want to be maniacal and obsessive about the use of time; however, it is imperative that you understand the meaning of the statement "time not well utilized is time wasted." People also spend a lot of time on activities that do not even match up to their current goals. Most often, these individuals lack self-awareness and are usually too busy and too unproductive to care about aligning activities with these crucial objectives.

Time wasters include poor planning, perfectionism, and, usually, excessive social media. To beat this, be more conscious about time and how it is utilized. It is also essential to prioritize daily activities or goals. By creating a list with priorities placed at the top, it becomes easier to stay motivated while addressing what is considered the most critical first.

These are the first few steps to take when trying to master the skill of time management. Next, try to align specific daily goals or plans with marked out periods of the day. It usually works, especially when you are deliberate about it.

For individuals who get quickly get distracted or are quick to forget things, reminders are an excellent way to go. These could be in the form of sticky notes placed on strategic, unmissable places. Digital devices would also be useful in this case with pop up notifications serving as reminders. Basically, prioritize and schedule tasks into your calendar.

Procrastination is another bad habit that prevents timeliness. Some individuals appear to do well under the pressure, stress, and nose-grinding effects of procrastination. To these people, procrastination is much like an extended incubating process, something like an "embryo state" right before work starts. However, as soon as they sight a deadline, they struggle to be productive amidst this energy-zapping process.

While procrastination almost always includes late arrival, stress, hurry, and unpreparedness, incubation remains a creative, subconscious process. It merely involves setting a problem aside for some time, in order to be able to generate better solutions.

To beat procrastination, get things done at the right time. Other ways to make doing things at the ideal time more comfortable, include shifting deadlines backward or employing the use of incentives.

Be ready

What comes to mind when you see the word ready? Proper organization? A clear sense of direction? Confidence, or a relaxed and calm state? That's precisely what preparedness, adequate management, and the dearth of procrastination do. Is it easy to differentiate a well-prepared presenter from an ill-prepared one? What are the signs? Fidgety behavior, a lack of organization, anxiety, or nervousness?

These are reasons to avoid being unprepared. Unpreparedness tends to have a ripple effect. It can lead to stress. Usually, when stress-related hormones are released, symptoms like anxiety come in next. For an entrepreneur, it becomes pretty difficult to make right decisions with such mind and mental states.

Show up early

Time is an indispensable resource. Showing up early connects well with preparedness, it is also usually perceived or interpreted as respect for people and their time. Depending on what has to be done, being early provides the opportunity for clarity, premeditation, and more productivity.

I usually arrive early to work, especially on days when meetings have been slated. After my first coffee cup, I do a quick overview of whatever's going to be discussed in the conference. Then, I go right ahead to catch up on the tasks

I have prioritized for the day. With this, I am better able to efficiently organize all the resources required for the tasks ahead, sometimes even accomplishing unrelated mini-tasks along the way.

Those few minutes gained are never less than productive for me. In my opinion, on time is late. This statement holds, especially when dealing with the unexpected. We cannot always predict how things turn out. However, by being early, we have a better shot at dealing with the unprecedented.

CHAPTER 6

TAKE ACTION

"You don't have to be great to start, but you do have to start to be great". -Zig Ziglar.

Do not just talk about it, create a blueprint of what's to be done, and then fail to take action. You have to do the necessary work, even if it involves positioning yourself in a "get things done or nothing" mind or mental state. To execute means to carry out or put things into effect. It involves deliberate effort and is seldom characterized by randomness. Many people find it difficult to get past the initial inertia when they have to accomplish a task or take action towards their goals.

My go-to solution for the problem can be summarized into; leveraging on support systems, incentivizing oneself and practicing working backward. Support systems want the best for you; they are the family, friends, and mentors who care and are committed to your progress. Often, they don't mind having to sacrifice their time and other resources to better improve your chances of success.

These individuals are like conscious cheerleaders on standby, always available to cheer their team. With them, there's little chance for inertia taking over with its debilitating effect. Mentorship also helps to beat inertia, mostly because a mentor is a guiding hand, a role model or expert who knows what next to do and how best to go about it. A mentor does this by sharing vital information and knowledge about his or her career path.

The mentor/mentee relationship is beneficial to execution or taking action because it provides the guidance, emotional support and motivation needed for a great start. For some people, the presence of an authority figure is the exact push that they need.

Perfectionism can also be a reason for final execution being hindered. To a perfectionist, there's always something to improve on, and some unmissable flaw hiding somewhere.

When I notice these tendencies within myself, I prefer to be held accountable to somebody else and not myself. What this does is take power away from me. Also, by setting clear rules and setting only realistic goals, I am able to beat my perfectionistic tendencies. It does not translate to lower standards; it simply gets the work done.

How does incentivization work? People do this in diverse ways, mainly by strategically rewarding themselves after reaching a target or milestone. Sticking with habits, tasks, and goals can be difficult, especially when the results are not quick to manifest. When people have something to look forward to, they are spurred on to take immediate action.

These could be rewards centered on fun and entertaining activities such as going out to see a movie, playing games, or listening to music.

Also, there are self-care, food, shopping, travel, and outdoors, as well as freestyle rewards. When planning out the best incentive, ensure that it matches up with the task to be accomplished. It is also best to be strategic about things. Do not select incentives that only serve to derail your goals.

Perseverance

Perseverance refers to persistence in the course of action, regardless of discouragement, possible opposition, or previous failure. It takes quite a lot to stick to goals and visions, especially when things do not seem to be working out well. It can be frustrating, and this is exactly why a visual and mental image of the desired result can go a long way to inspire motivation. Remember the practice of mentally walking backward to achieve your goals? That's an excellent place to start.

To leverage this, connect with a support system and be open to mentorship. Willpower doesn't always cut it. I always say it; perseverance is a key habit that's persistent in stories of great people who are known for achieving groundbreaking things. Henry ford, Thomas Edison, Walt Disney, Albert Einstein, Harriet Williams and Bethany

Hamilton, to mention a few; nobody ever became anything

tangible by succumbing to failure and setbacks.

CHAPTER 7

ORGANIZE

Organization is key to all areas of life. It refers to the way in which something is organized or the quality of being organized. Whatever is organized becomes structured, ordered, or operated by some principle or idea. Notable advantages of organization within the workplace include; improved efficiency, optimum utilization of resources, increased expansion and growth as well as overall effectiveness.

Systems and Strategies

Systems are a set of principles or procedures which instruct how a thing is done. They can also be described as interrelated entities that connect to form a unified whole. Systems relate to organization; they make up the parts that are usually integrated for specific goals to be accomplished. To incorporate systems thinking into your business, judge organizational groups based on their performance.

Organizational groups are a product of the identification and effective division of work. Usually, cohesive groups possess high morale and communicate better—fragmented groups; on the other hand, experience the opposite. Without peaceful interdependence and cohesiveness within a group, productivity reduces drastically. Regular assessment of workgroups within the company should be done regularly. The knowledge, skills, values, practices, and assigned duties of each workgroup should also be documented.

Usually, a systems analysis examines each workgroup's strengths and weaknesses and determines whether changes need to be made. These changes could involve a change in work allotted or reorganization within workgroups. After the process of systems analysis, there are vital things to note and takeaway. When the right questions are asked, various workgroups are better able to make the necessary adjustments and this fosters cohesiveness and increased productivity.

An organizational strategy can be described as those actions that have to be taken for a business or company to achieve a long-term goal. The larger part of a company's organizational strategy is usually spearheaded by top management. As a result of the trickledown effect, middle and low management adjust by adopting specific goals and objectives that would lead to the accomplishment of the overall strategy.

It can be likened to a journey that entails bits of step by step processes. A company's organizational strategy is usually generated from its mission statement.

Automation, tools, and resources

Automation is vital to organization. Think of how miserable we would be without basic forms of automation, such as email messaging? Automated tools aid the seamless distribution of information without the need for multiple systems. Redundant, monotonous tasks can also be accomplished without a thought. Leveraging automation and IT in business can reduce time wastage and improve productivity.

Automation is a growth-driving tool that can also help to increase accountability. My go-to organizational tools in the workplace include google keep, Trello, ClickUp, Hubspot CRM, Asana, Dropbox, smarter time, goggle drive pocket, and to-do-ist, to mention a few. Not only are they efficient, but they can also help to enhance work performance. Digital assistants, such as Siri or Cortana, are also a great choice.

CHAPTER 8

SAY NO

The word "No" is pretty powerful, even as powerful as its counterpart, Yes. However, we are mostly more fluid and freer with our use of the word yes compared to "No." We have been molded into being more open-minded. To us, Yes equals liberation, access to opportunities, no to fears of failure, and our given consent to make things happen. On the other hand, no, involves doors been shut, or some sort of negation, denial, disagreement, or removal of consent that's much needed for some action to occur.

The negativity that is perceived along with the word "No" is precisely why many people have a hard time saying it. They cannot stand to disappoint people or watch reactions to their use of the word no. So, these individuals tend to say a lot of yes. It's really not difficult to imagine the issues that arise from being a yes-woman or yes-man. Individuals who are not selective about what they choose to say yes to, that is, individuals who are not strategic with their no's tend to be regarded as people pleasers.

People who do not learn to say no end up being overwhelmed. In a bid to show up for their colleagues, family or friends, get these and that sorted out, they end up juggling way too much on their plates. The effects; unproductivity, not enough time for oneself, stress, and often disappointment. When these individuals get swamped with work and overwhelmed, they end up doing what it is they were avoiding in the first place, that is, disappointing people.

How do you make this work? When I feel bad about having to say no to anyone around me, my go-to strategy is reassuring myself that I've simply said yes to something else. It does not make me selfish. Usually, I'm the go-to person when my friends need help. However, instead of moping around and feeling guilty about having to say no, or saying yes and being overwhelmed later, I internalize the fact that my no simply is a yes to something else, something that is absolutely important to me.

Practice being assertive with the word "no" by utilizing anchor phrases that indicate an answer that would not be open for debate. For me, this would come in handy when dealing with sales persons, cashiers or strangers looking to pitch for profit. Normalizing saying no almost as reflexively as saying the yes word, would be great especially in more pressuring situations.

Don't want to be at the event? Be sure to let the person know as soon as you can in the politest way possible. Then, utilize that free time to get things done. It doesn't even have to be work; you could rest or engage in a relaxing activity. Learn to say no.

Tune out distractions

What are distractions? A distraction is anything that diverts attention from whatever's in focus, a goal, vision, or task ahead. These days we get the most distraction from the internet, social media, and digital devices. We are bombarded by ads and never-ending, constantly upgraded marketing strategies. In order to efficiently navigate this, scheduling is vital. Have phone rules addressing the amount of time spent on social media, as well as your availability to respond to emails. Utilize this extra time on something more productive and focus on profit-producing or money-making activities.

Negativity

When I feel negative thoughts swirling around my head, I meditate. Meditation provides clarity; with it, I find that I am better able to dissect my thoughts and feelings. Other useful activities that can serve to clear the mind include taking a walk or napping. The explosion of media outlets characterized these last few decades. We are constantly barraged by information on tv, on our phones, radio and billboards. Usually, this occurs with a lot of negativity. To deal with this, set up an information filter. I would not advise a total unplugging, instead be deliberate about what makes up your feeds.

Asides from virtual information, the people around you matter too. As social beings, we are able to pick up cues from other people. Depending on how receptive we are, it is possible to absorb negative energy. So, cut unnecessary ties and befriend only people who reciprocate your positive energy.

Negative thoughts are often temporary. However, when they become habitual, see a therapist.

CHAPTER 9

BE GRATEFUL

Gratitude can be described as being appreciative and thankful. It involves being thankful for where you are and what you have. It can be practiced; it is a state of being that embraces a journey or process without complaints. Gratitude does not preclude experiencing setbacks, failure, anger, or resentment. What is peculiar about it is the ability to set those aside and be more geared up for positivity.

There are multifarious advantages of gratitude. Individuals who practice being grateful until it becomes an ingrained habit have been reported to have higher levels of positive emotions and optimism. Expressing gratitude is key to happiness and increased life satisfaction; people who are continually grateful for what they have are less likely to place the utmost importance on material goods or be consumerists.

They have also been found to be more generous, empathetic, and helpful towards other people.

Gratitude is good for business; according to the Mindfulness Awareness Research Center, habitual gratitude changes the brain's molecular structure. It keeps the grey matter portion of the brain functioning while boosting serotonin and activating dopamine release. Being grateful is also linked to improved health and well-being.

Tips on practicing gratitude

- **Keep a gratitude journal**

A gratitude journal should contain a list of things you are thankful for. This simple but effective practice should be incorporated into morning and evening routines.

- **Connect with people you love daily.**

Ensure that your spouse, family members, and friends know how much you appreciate them. It does not have to be an overt display of affection if the situation does not warrant it. A little "thank you" would do. Be deliberate about it. Endeavor to spend quality time with them too.

- **Meditate with your gratitude list.**

Much like the affirmations repeated during meditation, affirming gratitude themed statements when meditating can bring a lot of positivity. Say things like, "I am thankful for my family and friends," "I'm grateful for the opportunity to see another day and make an impact today."

- **Commit to a designated "complain free" day**

This would require a blend of flexibility, patience, and understanding, knowing when to employ any of these is vital. Regardless of whatever happens, it is left to you to decide how to react. Begin the day with a firm resolution to avoid complaints and remain undisturbed, regardless of what the day brings.

- **Volunteer**

    Volunteering for the purpose of helping others is connected to increased well-being, overall health and happiness. It is a great way to offer essential aid to worthwhile causes, local communities, as well as charities. For some, volunteer activities also provide a sense of purpose. Usually, volunteering is a win-win situation that forms a positive feedback loop. It also ends up increasing our ability to be more grateful.

CHAPTER 10

MAINTAIN LIFE'S BALANCE

What comes to mind when you hear or see the word balanced? An undisturbed entity or settled body? A dangling pendulum? When I hear that word, it gets me thinking about peace. Peace with myself; that is, body, soul, and mind. Peace with the environment and the people around me as well. Balance refers to a state in which opposing forces harmonize, a state of equilibrium.

Often, when the question of "how to maintain life's balance" comes up, it is usually aimed at strategically navigating both work and family life. With a well-balanced life, personal effectiveness, peace of mind, and well-being are assured. A balanced life correlates with improved mood, reduced stress, and better health. Here are some tips on maintaining a well-balanced life.

Define your balance and what makes you happy

The three basic aspects to balance include work/business, family, and personal life. To be able to maintain a healthy balance amongst these various areas of life, passion for your work or job is essential. The primary aim of setting a balance is to be able improve well-being. However, it becomes hard to find an agreeable balance while being stuck in a restraining or draining job.

It is also nearly impossible to invest equal time in these listed areas. This is why it is absolutely essential to have a unique definition of the word "balance," that's peculiar to you. It could be 40:30:30 or whatever ratio is found fitting for a particular period.

Sometimes, something comes up, say, a new challenge at work or a family event to be planned for. Usually, this calls for immediate adjustments to be made on what is considered balanced. While flexibility is key, you must prioritize.

Prioritize

Along with examining your values and deciding what's most important to you, be organized. Prioritization and organization usually go hand in hand. When you have a strategic blueprint or a map that indicates your point of focus, you are likely to be better organized. Avoid trying to juggle too many activities at once; it is a well-known recipe for unproductivity, burnout, and failure.

Different life stages require different levels of commitment to various things. Some phases of life can be easily juggled or combined with others. However, some cannot be effectively managed. Basically, when making decisions, know what steps to take, how to take them, and which to put before the other.

Well-being matters

The common phrase is "health is wealth." Well-being describes a state of health, happiness or prosperity. It can be defined as the capacity to feel good and it is known to affect an individual ability to function effectively. High level of well-being is linked to productivity, resilience and stronger immunity. It is pretty impossible to attempt balancing the work-life routine with poor health. People who are unhealthy or have poor health will have a hard time utilizing their energy for multifarious purposes. Eat nutritious food, enjoy quality sleep, and do regular exercise. All these contribute to improved well-being and good health.